JAMES RIVER

RIVER

MISSOURI RIVER

Fort Kearny

Kearny Station (Hooks) Home Sta. (14)

Sand Hill (Summit)

32 Mile Creek (13)

(Lone Tree)(Spring Ranch)

Liberty Farm (12)

Oak Grove

Kiowa

Millersville

Big Sandy-Home Sta. (10)

Virginia City

Rock Creek (Lodi)(9)

Rock House (Caldwell)

Cottonwood (8)(Hollenberg)

Marysville-Home Sta. (7)

Guittard's

(Laramie Creek)(Hickory Point)

Seneca (5)

Log Chain (4)

Goteschall (Kickapoo)

Kennekuk (3)

Lewis (Cold Spring)

Troy

St. Joseph

S   R   O   U   T   E

-19-   -25-   -13-   -12-   -14-   -14-   -10-   -10-   -9-   -11- -10- -42-   -25-   -11- -14- -15-   -15- -14- -5-

SAS

KANSAS RIVER

Leavenworth•   •Fort Osage
                      •Independence

THE PONY EXPRESS
FROM ST. JOSEPH
TO FORT LARAMIE

by Merrill J. Mattes
and Paul Henderson

2162906

The Patrice Press
St. Louis, Missouri

Copyright © 1989
The Patrice Press

Library of Congress
Cataloging-In-Publication Data

Mattes, Merrill J.
    The Pony Express from St. Joseph to Fort Laramie /
by Merrill J. Mattes and Paul Henderson.
        p.   cm.
    Bibliography: p.
    ISBN 0-935284-66-4 : $4.95
    1. Pony express—History. 2. Terminals
(Transportation)—United States—History.
I. Henderson, Paul, b. 1895. II. Title.
HE6375.P65M226   1989
383'.143'0973—dc19   89-3325
                                                                  CIP

Front cover photo: Pony Express statue, St. Joseph,
   by Gregory M. Franzwa.
Back cover photo: Pony Express stables, St.
   Joseph, courtesy Pony Express Museum, 914
   Penn St., St. Joseph, MO 64501.

The Patrice Press
1701 S. Eighth Street
St. Louis MO 63104

Printed in the United States of America

Dedication
To the memory of two
splendid Nebraska trail historians:

Paul C. Henderson
1895-1979

Helen Henderson
1898-1988

CONTENTS

FOREWORD

Our enduring fascination with the West often focuses on events or episodes that have come to symbolize the nation's westering experience. The explorations of Lewis and Clark, the processions of emigrant wagons to Oregon and California, and Custer's debacle at the Little Bighorn are only a few. No list of the benchmarks of western history would be complete without the Pony Express. Its eighteen month saga captured the public's imagination in 1860-61; the Pony Express story remains vibrant and exciting today.

As the Pony Express centennial approached, Nebraska State Historical Society director William D. Aeschbacher noted the lack of an adequate history of the Pony Express across Nebraska. Accordingly, he asked two of the foremost authorities on the great Platte Valley route, Merrill J. Mattes and the late Paul Henderson, to prepare a study. Their article, based on extensive research and field trips to locate the sites of Pony Express stations, was published in *Nebraska History* 41, no. 2 (June, 1960). The article's popularity prompted its later reprint.

A steady flow of books, articles, and guides relating to the Oregon and California trails reflects an undiminished interest in the great highways of westward expansion. Recently the Oregon-California Trails Association was organized to promote the study and appreciation of these historic routes. Because the Pony Express forms an intriguing and dramatic chapter in the overland trail story, publication of a new revised edition of *The Pony Express from St. Joseph to Fort Laramie* is most appropriate. The Nebraska State Historical Society takes pleasure in joining with The Patrice Press in this endeavor.

James A. Hanson
Director
Nebraska State Historical Society

PUBLISHER'S FOREWORD

The decision of the Nebraska State Historical Society to limit their publication effort to their fine quarterly, *Nebraska History,* meant that this book, certainly one of the best on the Pony Express, would soon go out of print. They had kept the book in print for more than two decades; that was of great service to the community of history lovers who want to learn more about the famed mail service.

Our Patrice Press is pleased to have been selected to issue the book anew—this time with a greatly expanded pictorial offering. We relied heavily on James E. Potter of the Nebraska State Historical Society for guidance in the republication of the work; on the surviving co-author, Merrill J. Mattes; and especially on the former assistant director of the St. Joseph Museum, Don L. Reynolds. Reynolds, now retired from a lifetime of scholarship, devoted many years to the study of the Pony Express, and in fact read this manuscript twice to help update it.

Gregory M. Franzwa
March 1, 1989

About the authors:

Merrill J. Mattes, formerly chief preservation officer of the National Park Service, is retired and living in Littleton, Colorado.

His collaborator, Paul C. Henderson, lived in Bridgeport, Nebraska, and during his lifetime became the premier scholar on the geography of the Oregon Trail.

I.
INTRODUCTION [1]

The famed Pony Express lasted just eighteen months, from April 3, 1860, to October 24, 1861. It was a meteor, blazing through the skies of history, which burned out as the American Civil War began its thunderous barrage. The excitement which "the Pony" created in its own time was lost in the coming of transcontinental telegraph and the bellowing iron horse traversing the continent on shining rails.

In 1960-61, the Pony Express centennial created a new wave of excitement.

In an age when the continent can be spanned by jet planes in a few hours, and the near future holds

1. As the centennial of the Pony Express approached, the lack of an adequate, available narrative of the Pony Express in Nebraska occasioned the editor to ask Mr. Mattes to undertake a study. With the assistance of Mr. Henderson, Mr. Mattes has checked the available sources and compiled the following report. The authors state that in a true sense this is an "introduction" to the subject, and express the hope that it will call forth refinements of their introductory work.

Pony Express Saluting the Telegraph. Copied from the The Pacific Tourist, *1879.*

the realistic promise of a trip to the moon and beyond into the oceans of outer space—in such an age, the idea of relays of men on horseback seems quaint and antiquated. What, then, is the reason for the fascination of the Pony Express?

It is not in the stars but within ourselves that the answer lies. The Pony Express rider is symbolic of the bold imagination, the daring enterprise, and the reckless courage which are the highest expressions of the American character. This has been admirably expressed by Arthur Chapman:

> The ''Pony'' was one of the outward expressions of a certain business audacity which was common . . . on the frontier. Men plunged, and if they lost, were game in defeat. . . . The Pony was a financial failure which can be translated in terms of glory.

Pony Express Rider Passing Telegraph Construction, *by William H. Jackson.*

The Pony Express seldom failed those who anxiously awaited its arrival. Like a shuttle it wove back and forth across a 2,000 mile loom. . . . What it wove into the pattern of American life will be admired as long as we care for such things as adventure, romance, and rugged devotion to duty.

It is not for mere sentiment that this nation cherishes its heroes, preserves its historic places, and seizes upon the anniversaries of events to celebrate the past. It is from a deep instinctive recognition that noble and inspiring patriotic traditions are the bands of steel that bind us together as a nation, and that when these traditions lose their force and meaning we will disintegrate, spiritually and politically.

It is fitting, therefore, that the National Pony Express Centennial Association and the postmaster general of the United States have joined forces to sponsor appropriate celebrations, climaxed by the actual re-enactment of Pony Express runs, east and west, between St. Joseph, Missouri, and Sacramento, California.

Although many individuals contributed to the idea of fast-horse relays to speed communications to California, the reality was brought about by William B. Russell, the imaginative and daring entrepreneur of the great freighting firm of Russell, Majors, and Waddell.

Russell, Majors, and Waddell, as a private venture beginning in April 1861, and as a federally sanctioned project beginning in July 1861, was the firm which backed the Pony Express project financially and bore the brunt of its disastrous losses. Other companies were involved as agents in the business and before the Pony Express came to a close in October 1861, Ben Holladay took over the management. Nevertheless, the great credit for the remarkable venture remains with William B. Russell, who conceived and executed the bold plan with the somewhat reluctant but nevertheless honorable backing of his partners, Alexander Majors and William B. Waddell.

It cost nearly $100,000 to put the Express in operation between St. Joseph and Sacramento. Something like five hundred horses of superior stamina, including Kentucky-bred horses and

Pony Express Changing Horses, *by William H. Jackson.*

California mustangs, were purchased for the arduous service at around $175 each, a figure far in excess of the $25 to $50 which would buy an ordinary horse in those days. Over eighty riders, ''young skinny fellows, unmarried,'' were employed at beginning wages of fifty dollars per month plus board. About 157 Pony Express stations were established, complete with station keepers, stables, animals, and equipment.

The earlier stations, which served stagecoach passengers and provided spare teams, were located at approximately twenty-five mile intervals so that almost fifty percent of the Pony Express stations were stage stations already established and seeing double duty. This left approximately ninety-five brand new Pony Express stations to be set up, since the limit of a horse going at top speed was about twelve to fifteen miles an hour. Generally speaking, therefore, every second Pony Express station was a previously established stage station. The others were new stations thrown together hurriedly and stocked for the new service.

At the outset, each rider rode three mounts for a total distance of around forty-five miles to a "home station." He would then carry the mail coming in the opposite direction to the previous home station. While at first it appeared that the home stations were at an average of forty-five to fifty miles apart, later, perhaps in the interest of economy, home stations were more nearly at ninety-mile intervals and the riders made six changes of mounts. From the testimony of the riders, there were great irregularities in the distances traveled. Occasionally an emergency situation would require one man to ride continuously for two hundred miles or more!

Mail was sent by the Pony originally for five dollars per half ounce, but later this figure dropped to two dollars and then to one dollar per half ounce. It was carried in four flaps in a leather *mochila* which was thrown over the Pony Express saddle at each relay station. The ponies started from St. Joseph and Sacramento on a once-a-week basis; later this was stepped up to twice a week.

The original goal was a mail delivery from terminus to terminus in ten days. In order to achieve

Pony Express rider pursued by Indians along the Sweet-water. Split Rock is in the distance in this painting by William H. Jackson.

this, Pony riders had to average nine or ten miles an hour across approximately 1,838 miles. The ponies sometimes achieved spurts of sustained speed of twenty miles an hour, but of course the average time was cut by the obstacles of terrain, adverse weather, Indians, and accidents. The fastest time on record, around seven days and seventeen hours, was recorded when a special relay was set in motion to deliver President Lincoln's inaugural address to California. In this connection the Pony Express is credited with being a very important factor in cementing the new state of California to the threatened Union in 1860-61.

Operational headquarters for the Pony Express were located at St. Joseph, Missouri; Salt Lake City, Utah; and Sacramento, California. There were five

Fording the Platte Near Red Buttes, *by William H. Jackson.*

major divisions on the line. A. E. Lewis was the superintendent from St. Joseph to Fort Kearny, and Joseph Slade was superintendent from Fort Kearny to Horseshoe Station, Wyoming.

In 1912 Robert Harvey of the Nebraska State Historical Society and president of the Oregon Trail Commission made the first systematic effort to identify stage stations, Pony Express stations, and the general course of the Oregon-California Trail through Nebraska. A by-product of this survey was the line of monuments marking the trail and related sites.

Over the years other individuals have taken a keen personal interest in the problem of trail and

Nebraska State Historical Society

Overland Pony Express Pursed by Highwaymen. Copied from The Pacific Tourist, *1879.*

site identification. In the early 1930s Joseph G. Masters of Omaha and others collaborated on an effort to identify the old Pony stations. With the approach of the Pony Express Centennial in 1960, the writers gave serious thought to the problem of identifying Pony Express stations through Nebraska so that any centennial observances would be fitted within the framework of authentic scholarship.

In October 1959 a field trip was made over the trail between Fort Kearny and the Wyoming line. Available data were further analyzed and additional interviews conducted with people having specialized knowledge of the subject. Among these were Harry Williams and Paul Jenkins of Gothenburg; Mr.

The Pony Express monument displayed at many stations.

Warren Doolittle of North Platte; and John Oliver of Bridgeport, Nebraska. The results of the field trip and interviews were combined with information from sources listed in the next section.

II.
ANNOTATED PONY EXPRESS
BIBLIOGRAPHY [2]

Allen, O. *Allen's Guide Book and Map to the Gold Fields Of Kansas and Nebraska.* Washington, 1859.

This rare guide book includes reference to the numbered sequence of "U. S. Mail Stations" which existed under the government contract with Hockaday and Liggett, taken over by William B. Russell (as Jones, Russell and Company) in May 1859. Often referred to in Section III. Basis for column 2 of Section IV.

Andreas, A. T., ed. *History of the State of Nebraska.* Chicago, 1882.

Early county histories, with glimpses of places and events along the overland route.

---

2. In constructing this paper the need for a listing of Pony Express literature became apparent. Since repetitious footnotes from the same sources threatened to slow the narrative of the paper, this annotated bibliography plus the fourth section were put in to replace footnotes.

Bloss, Roy S. *Pony Express—The Great Gamble.* Berkeley, California, 1959.

A warmed-over treatment of material pioneered by Bradley, Chapman and Settle. Has some excellent illustrations.

Bradley, Glenn D. *The Story of the Pony Express.* Chicago, 1913.

The best pioneer treatment of the subject, generally reliable, and with the advantage of proximity of the writer to eyewitnesses. It was reprinted as the "official Centennial history" by Waddell F. Smith, President, Pony Express Centennial Association.

Burton, Richard F. *City of the Saints and Across the Rocky Mountains to California.* London, 1861.

One of the greatest classics of travel up the Platte River route, by an English gentleman adventurer with a vivid imagination and an addiction to classical allusions. Burton is a primary source on Pony Express stations. Of particular value is his "Emigrants' Itinerary" in the Appendix, compiled from his diary, "showing the distances between camping-places, the several mail-stations where mules are changed, the hours of travel, the character of the roads. . . . " Often referred to in Section III.

Carrington, Margaret I. *Ab-Sa-Ra-Ka, Land of Massacre: Being the Experience of an Officer's Wife on the Plains.* Philadelphia, 1879.

In 1866 the author accompanied her husband westward. She affords vivid descriptions of various establishments which were the Pony Express stations of 1861.

Chapman, Arthur. *The Pony Express: The Records of a Romantic Adventure in Business.* Chicago, 1932.

One of the most satisfying treatments of the subject. Contains interviews with Pony Express riders.

Clark, C. M., M. D. *A Trip to Pike's Peak.* San Jose, California, 1958.

Another traveler of 1860, he throws a few rays of light on the "ranches" or stations along the Pony route as far as Julesburg.

Conkling, Roscoe and Margaret B. *The Butterfield Overland Mail, 1857-1869: Its organization and operation over the Southern Route to 1861; subsequently over the Central Route to 1866; and under Wells Fargo and Company in 1869.* 3 vols. Glendale, 1947.

Especially chapter on Overland Mail on the Central Route, and Appendix J : *Stations on Original Central Route of Overland Mail Company in 1861 (Route No. 10773),* from U.S. Congress. Senate. 46th Cong., 3rd sess. S. Doc. 1, no. 21:7-8.

Dawson, Charles. *Pioneer Tales of the Oregon Trail and Jefferson County.* Topeka, 1912.

A rare and exceptionally informative county history which places the magnifying glass on a section of the Pony route in southeastern Nebraska. Several references in section III.

Denny, James. "A Trip to Pinpoint Pony Express Stops." *Omaha World-Herald.* Nov. 1, 1959.

A report on the Mattes-Henderson effort to retrace the Pony Express route and locate station sites between Fort Kearny and the Wyoming line.

Ellenbecker, John G. Letter to Paul Henderson on questions concerning Pony Express Route. Several references in Section III.

Franzwa, Gregory M. *Maps of the Oregon Trail.* St. Louis: Patrice Press, 1982.

Frederick, J. V. *Ben Holladay, the Stage Coach King.* Glendale, 1940: 46-68.

Discussion of the Central Overland Route.

Gilman, Musetta. *Pump on the Prairie.* Detroit: Harlo Press, 1975.

Gray, John S. "Fact vs. Fiction in the Kansas Boyhood of Buffalo Bill." *Kansas History* 8, no. 1 (Spring 1985).

Hafen, LeRoy R. *The Overland Mail, 1849-1869: Promoter of Settlement, Precursor of Railroads.* Cleveland, 1926: 165-95.

A scholarly, thoroughly documented analysis of the subject.

Harvey, August F. "A New Map of the Principal Routes to the Gold Regions of Colorado Territory." 1862.

A contemporary road map which identifies establishments on the "Denver Road" coinciding with the Pony Express through lower Nebraska. Referred to in Section III.

Harvey, Robert, and Addison E. Sheldon. "The Oregon Trail; Monuments and Markers in Nebraska." Report of their locations and inscriptions from a survey made during the years 1917 to 1923.

Typed manuscript in Nebraska State Historical Society library.

Henderson, Paul. "The Story of Mud Springs." *Nebraska History* 32, no. 2 (June 1951): 108-20.

Long, Margaret. *The Oregon Trail.* Denver, 1954.

This is a handbook for dedicated trail fans.

Majors, Alexander. *Seventy Years on the Frontier.* Chicago, 1893.

One of the founders of the Pony Express vividly recalls "The Pony Express and Its Brave Riders."

Masters, Joseph G.; Harry L. Williams; Paul Henderson; and Donald E. Prather. "Pony Express Stations in Nebraska." MS., ca. 1935. Nebraska State Historical Society.

An earlier effort to identify the Pony stops across Nebraska.

Mattes, Merrill J. "The Sutler's Store at Fort Laramie." *Annals of Wyoming* 18, no. 2 (July 1946): 93-138.

Documented study of a famous building, still standing, which dates back to 1849 and which was associated with the Pony Express in its heyday.

-----"Chimney Rock on the Oregon Trail." *Nebraska History* 36, no. 1 (March 1955).

-----"Fort Mitchell, Scotts Bluff, Nebraska Territory." *Nebraska History* 33, no. 1 (March 1952).

-----*The Great Platte River Road.* Lincoln: University of Nebraska Press, 1969.

National Archives. Natural Resources Division. Odometer Book from Fort Kearny, South Pass, and Honey Lake Wagon Road Expedition. 1857 (unpublished).

National Archives. Record Group No. 28 Postmaster General's Order and accompanying data relating to Route 10.773 of the Overland Mail Company, dated March 12, 1861, modifying the contract with that company for route 12.518, executed September 16, 1857.

"The Pony Express Rides Again." *Kansas Historical Quarterly* 25, no. 4 (Winter 1959):369-85.

Checklist of Kansas stations and digest of contemporary newspaper accounts.

Root, Frank A. and William E. Connelley. *The Overland Stage to California*. Topeka, Kansas, 1901.

Frank Root's personal reminiscences of his first overland trip as a mail messenger in 1863. The stage stations he describes are two years older than the Pony stations of 1861, but they are still the same stations. His dissertation on ''The Overland Pony Express,'' reflecting personal acquaintance with some of their riders, is a classic. Much used in Section III.

Settle, Raymond W., and Mary Lund Settle. *Saddles and Spurs: The Pony Express Saga*. Harrisburg, Pa., 1955.

Perhaps the best and most reliable of recent works on the subject, especially on background material.

Shumway, Grant L. *History of Western Nebraska and Its People*. Lincoln, 1921.

In the early pre-settlement phases, including Pony Express data, of doubtful reliability.

Twain, Mark. *Roughing It*. New York, 1871. Vol. I, 52-54.

A magnificent and oft-quoted description of a Pony rider in action near Scotts Bluff.

Ware, Eugene F. *The Indian War of 1864*. Kansas, 1911.

Ware is one of the most alert and intelligent observers of military posts, stations, and landmarks along the Platte River route in the early 1860s.

III.
PONY EXPRESS STATIONS, ST. JOSEPH TO FORT LARAMIE[3]

MISSOURI STATION NO. 1—St. Joseph: "St. Joe," as the eastern terminus of the transcontinental line, was of course a home station. The general office of the Pony Express was located in the Patee

---

3. To give continuity and unity to the Nebraska section the stations are listed from St. Joseph to Fort Laramie, two outstanding features of the trail. The following Pony Express structures still stand along this part of the trail.

St. Joseph—Both Patee House and Stables
Log Cabin—Rising's cabin, altered
Marysville—Restored as a museum
Cottonwood—Hollenberg Ranch, unaltered
Willow Island—altered and relocated in Cozad
Midway—unaltered
Machette's—altered and relocated in Gothenburg
Fort Laramie—Sutler's Store

All station names on the first line of an entry are from the mail contract of 1861. If the station was not on the mail contract the most common name appears in parenthesis.

Patee House in 1864. The hotel was also the Union provost marshall's office during the Civil War. The building is now a museum.

House, the town's most celebrated hostelry. This structure is still standing and today is an extensively equipped historical museum.

Perhaps even more expressive of the Russell, Majors, and Waddell enterprise is the "Pony Express Stable," generally accepted as an authentic survivor of the exciting days of 1860-61. This structure, located on the south edge of Patee Park opposite 912 Penn Street, is reputed to have been built by Benjamin Holladay in 1859, used by the Central Overland California and Pikes Peak Express Company as a base for its Pony riders. Gutted by fire in 1879, the walls remained over the decades, and in recent years the structure has been restored by

The Kansas State Historical Society, Topeka

Garrett Hollenberg's ranch house served as a home station for the Pony Express. It is located just northeast of Hanover, Kansas, and is open to the public.

the Goetz Pony Express Foundation. It is now managed by the St. Joseph Museum.

The spirit of the Pony Express finds expression is a magnificent statue of a Pony Express rider which stands in front of the City Hall.

Riders out of "St. Joe" had only a brief gallop to the wide Missouri River, over which they were conveyed by ferry boats. At the time of the Pony there were two steam ferries in operation, with Bellemont and Elwood on the Kansas side as their respective destinations. (The modern traveler crosses the river by bridge on U. S. 36, leaving Missouri close to the former ferry terminal.)

KANSAS STATION NO. 1—Elwood and/or Wathena: These towns (which are still in existence), are respectively about five and seven miles west of St. Joseph, and both are on the south side of a Missouri River bend. Each claimed a station. The *Elwood Free Press* of April 21, 1860, identifies Elwood as a station and this claim is supported by Allen and Long. A Pony Express monument which once graced U.S. 36, one-half mile south of Elwood, disappeared in the great Missouri River flood of 1952.

According to John Ellenbecker of Marysville, Kansas, Pony riders used the Bellemont ferry and landed at Wathena (now well inland, but in 1860 apparently on the river's edge). From there the rider used the old Pottawatomie trail for forty-two miles to Kennekuk where it was joined by the Leavenworth City Road. It is doubtful that either Elwood or Wathena was a bona fide relay station since the first certain station (Troy) is only fifteen miles from St. Joseph, the distance of the average ride per pony. Further, no station between St. Joseph and Troy was indicated in the U.S. Mail contract. It is possible that the company had an agent on the Kansas side to make certain that the mail got off to a good dryland start. This would constitute a ''station'' of sorts but not a relay station. Such an agent could have been at either Elwood or Wathena.

KANSAS STATION NO. 2—Troy: A monument standing in the northwest corner of the court house lawn is thought to be at the site of the original relay station. The old stage road out of St. Joseph via Elwood junctioned at Troy with the old Pottawatomie trail that crossed via the Bellemont ferry. Burton describes the Troy of 1860 as "a few wretched shanties."

KANSAS STATION NO. 3—Lewis: This site may have been in Sec. 19, T4S, R19E, but has not been definitely located. The "Lewis" on the mail contract suggests the name of the stable proprietor. This may have been the "Chain Pump" of Allen or the "Valley Home" of Burton, but if so he errs in placing it ten miles from Troy. A rival claimant for Kansas Station No. 3 is "Cold Springs," which Ellenbecker places on North Independence Creek Sec. 36, T3S, R19E, near present Severance.

KANSAS STATION NO. 4—Kinnekuk: Except for variations in spelling (Kennekuk, Kenykirk), there is general agreement on the identity and location of this station in the middle of Sec. 3, T5S, R17E. Kinnekuk was a rather substantial settlement, boasting a dozen houses, a store, a blacksmith shop, and the Kickapoo Indian Agency. A stone monument marks the site, one and one-half miles southeast from present Horton. This was the first home station, forty-four miles from St. Joseph, and the junction point with the Fort Leavenworth-Fort Kearny Road.

Don Reynolds

This boulder marks the site of the Kinnekuk station.

KANSAS STATION NO. 5—Goteschall: Again there is a general agreement on the location of this station, more commonly known as "Kickapoo." The identified site is on Delaware (Plum or Big Grasshopper) Creek, in Sec. 14, T4S, R15E about twelve miles east of Horton. The old stone Kickapoo Indian Mission building of 1851, one mile northwest of the Pony station, was also used as a hotel for stage passengers.

KANSAS STATION NO. 6—Log Chain: This station is in Sec. 19, T3S, R14E, on Locknan's or Muddy Creek, just outside the western border of the Kickapoo Indian reservation. "Log Chain" may commemorate the frequent snapping of chains as wagons were driven across the difficult creek bed, as legend has it. More likely, it is a corruption of the stream name, which in turn appears to have been named for an otherwise mysterious early settler or innkeeper. Proprietor N. H. Rising's barn has disappeared but a 24 X 40 foot log cabin, somewhat altered and now covered with boards, is now believed by the Kansas State Historical Society to be a Pony Express original. Ellenbecker and others erroneously identify old Granada, four miles south of here, as the station.

KANSAS STATION NO. 7—Seneca: This important home station was on the headwaters of the Nemaha River. It was a famous hotel kept by John E. Smith and noted among stage passengers for its

Smith's Hotel, Seneca, Kansas, was demolished in 1972.

A drawing of Smith's Hotel, Seneca, Kansas. Copied from The Overland Stage To California, *by Root and Connelley, Topeka, 1901.*

fine food. The old building, which served many years as a private residence in the town of Seneca (on U. S. 36), was torn down in September 1972. The original site at the corner of Main and Fourth Street is identified by a boulder with inscription.

KANSAS STATION NO. 8—Ash Point: Identification is confirmed in the SW corner, SE ¼, Sec. 8, T2S, R11E, on Vermillion Creek, two miles northeast of Axtell, on U. S. 36. A granite monument placed by Ellenbecker commemorates the site. The well dug by station keeper O'Laughlin was recently found near a lone tree, covered with flat stones. Ash Point had three aliases—Frogtown or Laramie Creek (Root and Connelley) and Hickory Point (Allen). A monument stands three-fourths of a mile west of the site.

The ''Uncle John's Grocery'' cited by Burton was probably a separate site.

KANSAS STATION NO. 9—Guittard's: It was at Guittard's that Burton saw his first Pony Express rider. This station, once operated by the George Guittard family, is pinpointed in the SW corner, SW ¼, Sec. 2 T1S, R9E. The site, one-fourth of a mile east of a marker on the east side of a county road, is to the north of the hamlet of Beattie. This was also called Vermillion Creek station.

The ''Oketo Cutoff'' from Guittard's to Rock House or Otoe Station just across the Nebraska line, crossing the Big Blue River north of Marysville,

St. Joseph Museum

Guittard Brothers, left, and Joseph Thoman.

Don Reynolds-St. Joseph Museum

The Overland Stage left this deep, eroded groove near Guit-
tard's station.

Don Reynolds-St. Joseph Museum

Farm buildings now at the site of Guittard's station.

Mrs. Xavier Guittard, left, and Madeline Guittard, daughter of Joseph Guittard, shown at the dedication of the Guittard station marker in 1930.

was not laid out for the stage line until 1862. Accordingly, it is not a proper part of the Pony Express story.

KANSAS STATION NO. 10—Marysville: This now substantial community, once known also as Palmetto City or Big Blue Station, was described by Burton as a "town which thrived by selling whiskey to ruffians of all descriptions." At 108 South Eighth

Thomas Ryan, the first Pony Express rider out of Marysville, Kansas.

The Kansas State Historical Society

The Marysville station looked like this in the 1960s, but has since been restored and now serves as a museum.

Street, the original Pony Express station still stands, where it spent many years well disguised as part of a modern cold storage plant. The station has since been restored and is now a museum. This was presumably a home station. The Pony riders used Marshall's ferry in crossing the Big Blue, and to the west a few miles from there joined the original Oregon Trail out of Independence, Missouri. This is eight and one-half miles above the old Independence ferry, near Alcove Springs, used by early Oregon emigrants. The Pony Express route now coincides with the classic Oregon Trail from here across Nebraska and past Fort Laramie.

KANSAS STATION NO. 11—Cottonwood: Here, in the SE corner, Sec. 3, T2S, R5E, one and one-half miles northeast of Hanover on a knoll overlooking Cottonwood Creek, is a small historical park operated by the Kansas State Historical Society. The original Cottonwood station in the park is open to the public. This venerable structure of rough-sawed lumber is also identified as the famous ranch of G. H. Hollenberg. A German emigrant, he had joined the gold rushes to California and Peru; later he served emigrants and stage lines at his ranch and became the first postmaster of Washington County.

NEBRASKA STATION NO. 1—Rock House: The Pony Express route entered Nebraska in the SW corner (T1N, R5E) of Gage County, crossing immediately northwestward into the SE corner of Jefferson County. Rock House station, where the later Oketo Cutoff rejoined the main Pony route, is in NE ¼ NW ¼ of Sec. 15, T1N, R4E, about three miles northeast of Steele City. It is called Otoe station by Root and Connelley.

NEBRASKA STATION NO. 2—Rock Creek: This station site, later to become notorious because of the infamous episode involving McCanles and ''Wild Bill'' Hickok, is north of the center of Sec. 26, T2N, R3E, Jefferson County, about six miles southeast of Fairbury. Other names for the station are Pawnee (Root and Connelley) and Turkey Creek (Burton). Nearby is old Whiskey Run Ranch,

St. Joseph Museum

Garrett H. Hollenberg, founder of the Cottonwood station, now preserved as the Hollenberg station, near Hanover, Kansas.

Veteran Pony Express sleuth Don Reynolds stands near a deep swale of the Oregon Trail near Rock Creek station.

Quivera Park with a Fremont inscription, and sandstone outcrops with many carved emigrant records.

According to Dawson's *History of Jefferson County,* in 1859 McCanles built a toll bridge over Rock Creek and a ranch on the east bank of the stream, which structure became the Pony station. This was built of hewn logs 36 feet long, 16 feet wide and 8 feet high at the eaves, with a large stone fireplace and attic reached by outside stairway. [Rock Creek station has been authentically restored and is now administrated by The Nebraska Game and Parks Commission as a State Historical Park.]

NEBRASKA STATION NO. 3—Virginia: This site lies four miles north of Fairbury, in the NE corner, Sec. 27, T3N, R2E. Other names used are Grayson's (Root and Connelley) and Whiskey Run (Allen). Lone Tree, in the middle of the SW ¼ of Sec. 35, one mile south of Virginia, crops up as an alternate site.

NEBRASKA STATION NO. 4—Big Sandy: This was an important home station. The site lies within the SW ¼ of Sec. 16, T3N, R1E, about three miles east of Alexandria, Jefferson County. The Nebraska City Road joined the Oregon Trail a short distance west of Big Sandy. According to Dawson, the owner and operator of the station was Dan Patterson, who in 1860 sold it to Asa and John Latham. Also associated with this site are the ranches of Ed Farrell and a Daniel, the latter a post office.

NEBRASKA STATION NO. 5—Millersville: This site, about 3.2 miles northeast of Hebron, approximately five miles southwest of Alexandria, in Thayer County, was operated by George B. Thompson and is called Thompson's station by Root and Connelley. [Using information available in the late 1980s, the station's location has been pinpointed in NE ¼ of NW ¼ Sec. 28.]

NEBRASKA STATION NO. 6—Kiowa: This site, in the SE corner NE ¼ of Sec. 16, T3N, R4W, about ten miles northwest of Hebron, Thayer County, had Jim Douglas as the station keeper. The old trail reached the Little Blue River about one mile east of this station and followed along its left bank to beyond Spring Ranch.

NEBRASKA STATION NO. 7—Oak Grove: The mail contract for 1861 indicated but did not name this station. This is the first Nuckolls County station, the site being about one and one-fourth miles southeast of Oak, in the NW ¼, Sec. 15, T3N, R5W. Al Holliday served as the station keeper, while a ''Majors & Waddell Store'' was reported to adjoin. Little Blue station, four miles northwest, was probably a later stage station. Among contemporary ranches in this vicinity were Roper's, Emory's and Eubank's. E. S. Comstock owned the Oak Grove ranch. In August 1864 this neighborhood was terrorized by Sioux.

NEBRASKA STATION NO. 8—Liberty Farm: The origin of this interesting name is obscure. The site of this home station is within the NE ¼ Sec. 32, T5N, R7W, just one-half mile northeast of Deweese in Clay County, on the north bank of the Little Blue. It is marked by Nebraska Monument No. 26. In 1859 Allen reported: ''Jct. of Ft. Riley Road 19 miles from Oak Grove, U.S. Mail station No. 12. 1 ½ miles east of this place.'' This junction is marked by Nebraska Monument No. 26 ½. Successive station keepers in 1860-61 are named as James Lemmons and Charles Emory. In 1864 Indians burned out J. M. Comstock here. Liberty Farm was succeeded by the Pawnee Ranch.

NEBRASKA STATION NO. 9—Spring Ranch: There was a Spring Ranch destroyed by Indians in 1864. Evidence is not conclusive that this was a Pony Express station since it is not mentioned in the mail contract, but it is in the logical spot distance-wise between Liberty Farm and Thirty-Two Mile Creek, a long twenty-five miles apart. It may coincide with the Lone Tree stage station of Root and Connelley. Nebraska Monument No. 29 places the ranch in the N ½ SE ¼ SE ¼, Sec. 8, T5N, R8W in Clay County. The trail left the Little Blue River a few miles beyond this point.

NEBRASKA STATION NO. 10—Thirty-Two Mile Creek: All agree on name and location in the NE ¼, Sec. 6, T6N, R10W, about six miles southwest of Hastings. A numberless Nebraska Monument marks the site as "Dinner Station, I.O.O.F.E., Pony Express." This was a long one-story building operated by George A. Comstock. It was abandoned after the 1864 raids.

NEBRASKA STATION NO. 11—Summit: Called "Water Hole" in Allen, and "Fairfield" in Chapman's interview with William Campbell. The site falls within the SE corner NE ¼, Sec. 10, T7N,

R12W, one and one-half miles south of Kenesaw, on the crest of the divide between Little Blue and Platte River drainages. In 1863 it was described by Root as "one of the most lonesome places in Nebraska." This station was another casualty of the Indian trouble in 1864.

NEBRASKA STATION NO. 12—Kearny Station: This was a home station, kept by M. H. Hook, and marked the end of the jurisdiction of E. A. Lewis, St. Joseph-Fort Kearny division superintendent. The site is found within the NE ¼, Sec. 18, T8N, R13W, about one and one-half miles northeast of present Lowell, Kearney County. Burton refers to "Kearney station, in the valley of LaGrande Platte," seven miles from the fort of that name. This station had numerous other identities, among them Dogtown or Valley City (Root and Connelley); Junction City (Andreas); and Hinshaw's Ranch (Harvey Map of 1862).

NEBRASKA STATION NO. 13—Fort Kearny: Although claims are made to this effect, it is improbable that Fort Kearny (spelled with two "e's" in the mail contract) itself had a Pony Express station. True, the Holladay Stage Line from St. Joe and the Western Stage Line from Omaha (via north side of the Platte and Carson's Crossing) made this fort itself a major objective, and in 1859 Holladay had a log structure "40 rods west of the fort." Pony riders conceivably paused here to pick up or deliver

Painting of Fort Kearny by William H. Jackson

occasional military or civilian mail, perhaps at the
sod post office structure erected in 1848. However,
it is more likely that the Pony station or stable itself
was at Doby Town, two miles west of the fort and
just off the reservation. This would be in Sec. 19
and 30, T8N, R15W, about five miles south and
east of present Kearney, on the right bank or
Oregon Trail side of the Platte. [The site of Doby
Town is on the National Register of Historic Places.]

NEBRASKA STATION NO. 14—Platt's: This station, which would be approximately five miles
southeast of Odessa, is named in the mail contract
and is spelled Platte by Root and Connelley.
The "Seventeen Mile Station" of Burton, where his

stage halted to change mules, may be identical with Platt's.

NEBRASKA STATION NO. 15—Garden: This was apparently the same as Craig Station of Root and Connelley and might also be the Biddleman Ranch that appears on the Harvey Map of Nebraska, 1862. It could also be the "Shakespear" that is indicated by Dr. Clark in 1860. Its exact location is not known, but *Maps of the Oregon Trail* places it on the line between sections 13 and 14, T8N, R19W. Apparently it was about six miles southwest of Elm Creek in Phelps County.

NEBRASKA STATION NO. 16—Plum Creek: All agree on the name and the place, the SW corner, Sec. 8, T8N, R20W, about ten miles southeast of Lexington. Nearby is an old cemetery where there are buried eleven victims of an Indian attack of August 8, 1864.

NEBRASKA STATION NO. 17—Willow Island: Allen offers the variant of Willow Bend. Burton refers to a "drinking shop at Willow Island Ranch." The site would be about nine miles southeast of Cozad, Dawson County, in the N ½, Sec. 8, T9N, R22W, near the south end of the Platte River bridge southeast of Darr. Some sources place Pat Mullaly's ranch and station at this site. R. C. Freeman, an employee of Mullaly, followed Mullaly as owner and operator of the ranch. The log cabin on the site was purchased by the Dawson County

Don Reynolds-St. Joseph Museum

Plaque on Willow Island Pony Express station, now in the city park in Cozad, Nebraska.

American Legion Post No. 77 and moved to the park in Cozad for the use of Boy Scouts. It was dedicated in September 1938 and marked with a plaque relating its history as a ranch on the Oregon Trail and as a Pony Express station.

NEBRASKA STATION NO. 18—Midway: This important home station survives to this day, in the NW ¼, Sec. 35, T11N, R25W, three miles south of Gothenburg, on the Harry Williams Ranch. The remarkable cabin, built of heavy adzed timbers, has been used until recently as a farmhand dwelling, but it has been carefully preserved by Williams, who appreciates its historic value. It has never been removed from its original location. [The cabin has been entered on the National Register of Historic Places.] It bears the circular bronze Pony Express plaque of the Oregon Trail Memorial Association, plus another bronze marker which states that on June 8, 1860, Pony rider Jim Moore rode from Midway to Julesburg, Colorado, and back in record time, in an emergency situation caused by Indian troubles. David Trout is named as station keeper as of 1863.

Midway received its name, Root and Connelley point out, because it was equidistant on the stage line between Atchison and Denver. It was also referred to as Heavy Timber (Allen), Smith's East Ranch (Harney Map of 1862), and Pat Mullaly's home station. Its location is now known as the Lower 96 Ranch.

St. Joseph Museum

Midway Pony Express station as it appeared in 1892

Gregory M. Franzwa

Midway station today

Gilman's Ranch station, now located in Gothenburg Park, Nebraska. It was used as an Overland Trail Stage station, dwelling, bunk house, and storage house on Upper 96 Ranch, four miles west of Fort McPherson, from 1862 to 1931. Built in 1854, it was donated to the city of Gothenburg, Nebraska.

NEBRASKA STATION NO. 19—Gilman's: This point is indicated by Root and Connelley and the U.S. mail contract. It is near the SW ¼, Sec. 4, T11N, R26W, in Lincoln County. [Musetta Gilman's delightful *Pump on the Prairie* offers a fine history of Gilman's Station.]

Blacksmith shop at Sam Machette's station

NEBRASKA STATION NO. 20—Machette's: This is a mystery station, the site being on the Williams' Upper 96 Ranch, Lincoln County, four miles east of Fort McPherson. It is not mentioned by Burton, Allen, Root and Connelley, or their published authorities, nor can ''Machette'' be identified in any available contemporary sources. However, there is the weight of local tradition, reflected in this wording on a monument in the SW corner, SE ¼, Sec. 19, T12N, R27W: ''Erected by the people of Lincoln County, 1931, to commemorate the Pony Express riders. This is one of the regular stations of the Pony Express. The log blacksmith shop nearby is the original building used for shoeing horses.'' [Musetta Gilman places Machette's in Sec. 14, T12N, R28W.]

St. Joseph Museum

Sam Machette Pony Express station before the building was dismantled and a portion moved to the city park in Gothenburg, Nebraska. The second story was added in the early 1880s.

Harry Williams stated that the indicated "blacksmith shop" still stands. A portion of a larger two-story squared log building which used to stand here, was donated by Mrs. C. A. Williams and moved in 1931 by the American Legion to the city park in Gothenburg, on U.S. 30, several miles east and on the north side of the Platte River, where it is now a tourist attraction. It was rebuilt as a one-story structure. The affixed tablet indicates that the original building was built in 1854 as a trading post and ranch house (by "Machette"?). In 1860-61 (the tablet explains) it was used as a Pony Express station; from 1862-1932 "as an overland station, dwelling, bunk house and storage house on Upper

96 Ranch.''

Along with the lack of contemporary records of Machette's, there is the fact that the Pony stations averaged fifteen miles apart, and it is just sixteen miles between Gilman's station and Cottonwood Springs or McDonald's station (see below), the authenticity of both of which is unimpeachable. What then was "Machette's" doing in between? The structure now in Gothenburg seems to have much in common with the doubtlessly authentic Midway structure. If of the same vintage, the answer could lie in supposing that Machette's was in existence in 1860-61 as a ranch. The name might be a corruption of "McDonald," and the Upper 96-Gothenburg structure could actually be the original McDonald's station, transplanted some time after the 1860s to the Upper 96.

NEBRASKA STATION NO. 21—Cottonwood Springs: This place, or "McDonald's Ranch," was another station on the Pony run and, like many others discussed here, doubled also as an Overland Stage station, being midway between Fort Kearny and Julesburg. The site, marked by a monument, is on the east side of Cottonwood Creek in the NW ¼, Sec. 15, T12N, R28W, on a gravel road less than one-half mile east of the later (1864) Fort Cottonwood, which became Fort McPherson, and one mile southeast of the present Fort McPherson National Cemetery. In 1860 Burton refers here to "the foul tenement" where he threw himself upon a mattress

The store and residence of Charles McDonald at Fort McPherson. It was located about ¼ mile east of the military post. This is how it looked in 1860.

to sleep; but in 1863 Root says that is was a "home station" and "nearly everything about the premises appeared homelike." In 1864 Eugene F. Ware reports:

Cottonwood Springs, when we arrived there, was one of the important points on the road. Mac-Donald had a year or so before our arrival, built, as stated, a cedar-log store-building. The main building was about twenty feet front and forty feet deep, and was two stories high. A wing 50 feet extended to the west. The latter was, at the eaves, about eight feet high and fifteen feet deep in the clear. Around it in the rear was a large and defensible corral, which extended to the arroyo coming out of the canyon. It had been a good trading-point with the Indians, and there was a stage station there, and a blacksmith shop kept by a man named Hindman. In the stage station was a telegraph office. There was also on the other side of the road a place where canned goods and liquors were sold, kept by a man named Boyer, who had lost a leg, and whom the Indians called "Hook-sah," which meant "cut leg." MacDonald had dug, in front of his store, and cribbed up, an inexhaustible well, which was said to be forty-six feet deep; it was rigged with pulley, chain, and heavy oaken buckets. MacDonald and those at the place had formerly had a good trade with the Indians, but now it was all ended, and they were in danger.

Here is a two-story log building, with appendages. (A photograph of this appears on page 64 of Ware.) The structure on the Upper 96 Ranch was a two-story log building. Again, it is suggested that these might be one and the same building, perhaps torn down and re-assembled at the latter point. It is not certain that the structure Ware describes was the 1861 Pony Express station, but it is a reasonable hypothesis, pending further revelations.

NEBRASKA STATION NO. 22—Cold Springs: This site, named by Root and Connelley, would be in Sec. 18, T13N, R30W, in the vincinity of Box Elder Creek, Lincoln County, fifteen miles west of Cottonwood Springs, and two miles south and one mile west of present North Platte. It is easy to confuse this station with Jack Morrow's ranch or ''Junction House'' (so named for its proximity to the forks of the Platte), which was twelve miles from Cottonwood. Root and Connelley clarify this point.

Masters has a Box Elder station ''three miles west of Cottonwood Springs,'' named by Sheldon Davis. This short distance would not admit a Pony station so close.

NEBRASKA STATION NO. 23—Fremont Springs: Although just when the explorer Fremont visited this site is another good mystery, the name was consistently used except by an obscure traveler of 1860, a Dr. Clark, who speaks of ''Buffalo Ranch.'' This is spoken of as a home station, which seems reasonable in view of the fifty-mile distance from Midway. This station was unlike its neighbors. According to Burton ''the building is of a style peculiar to the south, especially Florida—two huts connected by a roofwork of thatched timber, which acts as the best and coolest of verandahs.''

The site was located in the NW corner, Sec. 4, T13N, R32W, about one and one-half miles due south of Hershey.

NEBRASKA STATION NO. 24—Dansey's: There was an early Indian agent, Benjamin O'Fallon, for whom the Platte River bluffs here were inexplicably named. The mail contract refers to ''Dansey's,'' presumably the Pony Express proprietor. Burton had the inevitable trading post. Root and Burton both offer rather vivid descriptions of the unsavory establishment. Old Julesburg was a mighty busy place, primarily because it was at the junction of the main roads up the South and North Platte rivers respectively called the Pikes Peak or Denver Road, and the California Road or Overland Trail. The stages and the Pony Express used the latter route, here fording the South Platte (wide and rough in spring flood) to a point just above Lodgepole Creek, then following that stream westward to a point three miles west of present Sidney, then crossing Lodgepole and going north. This route was surveyed by Lieutenant Bryan of the Topographical Engineers in 1858 and was called "Jules Stretch." Old Julesburg was sacked by Sioux and Cheyenne in February 1865. The site of Fort Rankin (later Fort Sedgwick), a mile or so west of Old Julesburg, should be noted. The writers found no less than fifteen monuments scattered about this historic tip of northeastern Colorado.

NEBRASKA STATION NO. 28—Nine Mile: This te is in Sec. 26, T13N, R45W, two miles southeast f Chappell, in Deuel County.

NEBRASKA STATION NO. 29—Pole Creek No. 2: ddly enough, this is named in the U.S. mail con-ct, but no traveler has mentioned it. Its location ague, being in the vicinity of Lodgepole, roughly lfway on the twenty-four mile stretch between

speaks of "Half Way House" and Root and Connelley use "Elkhorn." In any event, the site is believed to be in the NE corner, SE ¼, Sec. 3, T13N, R34W, about two miles south and four miles west of Sutherland. Marvin Kivett says it is reported to be on the Nora Schuler Farm. Root describes the section embracing O'Fallon's Bluffs as "undoubtedly the best place between the Missouri River and Rocky Mountains for skulking Indians to hide."

NEBRASKA STATION NO. 25—Alkali Lake: Dr. Clark in 1860 calls this Pike's Peak station. The station is indicated but is given no name in the mail contract. Otherwise the name "Alkali Lake" is unanimous. The site, like others in this area, is not definitely located. It may be in the middle of Sec. 12, T13N, R37W, about seven miles southwest of Paxton, Keith County.

NEBRASKA STATION NO. 26—Gill's: This was the point of the Texas trail crossing of the 1870s. In 1860 it was called Gill's in the mail contract, but Sand Hill by Root and Connelley. Nobody else bothers to mention it; it was just another obscure relay station. Although its precise location is unknown, it was about one and one-half miles south of Ogallala, Keith County.

NEBRASKA STATION NO. 27—Diamond Spring: Nebraska's Monument No. 40, located .9 mile west of Brule, Keith County, on the south side of U.S.

Don Reynolds-St. Joseph Museum
Art Anderson at Diamond Springs Monument

30, reads: "Diamond Springs .8 mile southwest." This was probably a home station, though it is un comfortably close to Julesburg, which was also home station. The site has been tentatively locate as the SW corner, SE ¼, Sec. 21, T13N, R40 However, two miles west of this point, in NW Sec. 30, was the Beauvais Ranch, with buildi of hewn logs, which enjoyed considerable f through the 1850s and 1860s. With such an es lishment handy, why wouldn't it serve as a stat This question remains unanswered.

Beauvais is at one of the famous South River fords, variously identified as Lower ing, Ash Hollow Crossing, Fort Laramie Cr and Old California Crossing. The emigran crossed here went over the plateau to rea Hollow on the North Platte, but the Pony did not follow this route.

COLORADO STATION NO. 1—Frontz's: is marked two miles east of present Jules SE corner, NE ¼, Sec. 28, T12N, R44W, County. Variants are South Platte station (Connelley) and Butte station.

COLORADO STATION NO. 2—Julesb site, not to be confused with var Julesburgs, is the original Old Julesbur marked in NW ¼, NW ¼, Sec. 15, T1 one and one-half miles southeast of Ovi County. The place was named for Jule

Only traces remains of the Lodgepole station site, located on the Schnells' St. George Ranch east of Sidney, Nebraska. Faint ridges mark the location of buildings and corrals.

Nine Mile and Pole Creek No. 3. It is possible that it may be identical with the site of the ranch occupied hereabouts by E. Farrell in 1865.

NEBRASKA STATION NO. 30—Pole Creek No. 3: This site was on the north side of Lodgepole Creek, in the NE corner, NE ¼, Sec. 35, T14N, R49W, on the old St. George Cattle Ranch, about three and one-half miles east of Sidney, Cheyenne County. Old maps identify this as the stage ranch of Rouliette and Pringle, with well fortified buildings

part dugout, part sod and logs. The ford must have
been at or near this point. This place had impor-
tance as the junction of the old California Road and
stage route heading for the North Platte, and a new
stage route heading due west for Bridger Pass and
Salt Lake City. (This is the ''Lodgepole Route''
which later became the Union Pacific route to
Cheyenne.)

Burton's description of ''Lodgepole Station,''
although serving him as a stage station, may be
taken as a rare contemporary description of a
Nebraska Pony Express station:

> The hovel fronting the creek was built like an
> Irish shanty, or a Beloch hut, against a hill side,
> to save one wall, and it presented a fresh phase
> of squalor and wretchedness. The mud walls were
> partly papered with Harper's Magazine, Frank
> Leslie, and the New York Illustrated News; the
> ceiling was a fine festoon-work of soot, and the
> floor was very much like the ground outside, only
> not nearly so clean. In a corner stood the usual
> ''bunk,'' a mass of mingled rags and buffalo robes;
> the centre of the room was occupied by a rickety
> table, and boxes, turned-up on their long sides,
> acted as chairs. The unescapable stove was there,
> filling the interior with the aroma of meat. As
> usual, the materials for ablution, a ''dipper'' or
> cup, a dingy tin skillet of scanty size, a bit of coarse
> gritty soap, and a public towel, like a rag of gun-
> ny bag, were deposited upon a rickety settle

outside.

There being no "lady" at the station on Lodge-pole Creek, milk was unprocurable. Here, however, began a course of antelope venison, which soon told upon us with damaging effect.

[Burton was forever complaining about the terrible food at these stage stations.]

NEBRASKA STATION NO. 31—Unnamed: This station does not appear in official records, and the existence of something here is mentioned only by a Mrs. Carrington in 1866, who tells of a "Government well" to furnish water for the mail stations. Reconnaissance of the site has revealed evidence of structures. There had to be a relay station somewhere along the twenty-five miles between Pole Creek No. 3 and Mud Springs. The site located is within the Sioux Ordnance area, SE corner, Sec. 12, T15N, R50W, about three miles south and one mile west of Gurley on U.S. 385.

NEBRASKA STATION NO. 32—Mud Springs: This site is in the SW ¼, Sec. 31, T18N, R49W, about twelve miles southeast of Bridgeport in Morrill County. It is now within a one-acre tract of ground donated by Mrs. Etta A. Scherer as a state park. [The site is on the National Register of Historic Places.] This was a home station, the first since Julesburg. Archaeological search of the building remains confirms the ground plan made

MUD SPRINGS STATION
A STATION ON THE PONY EXPRESS ROUTE, 1860-1861.
A STATION ON THE FIRST TRANSCONTINENTAL TELEGRAPH
LINE, AND ON THE OVERLAND STAGE ROUTE.
BATTLE BETWEEN SIOUX INDIANS AND U.S. TROOPS
FEB. 6-7, 1865.
THIS SITE HAS BEEN GIVEN TO THE STATE OF NEBRASKA BY
ETTA H. SCHERER AND CHILDREN TO BE PRESERVED AS A
MEMORIAL TO ALL EARLY PIONEERS WHO WON THE WEST.
MONUMENT ERECTED JUNE 11, 1949 BY
The Mud Springs Womans Club

Don Reynolds-St. Joseph Museum

Marker at the Mud Springs station site

Don Reynolds-St. Joseph Museum

Pools remain at the site of Mud Springs Pony Express station.

of this site by Lt. Caspar Collins in 1864. The Pony station and the stage station are doubtless the same building. Troops from Fort Laramie occupied Mud Springs in February 1865, and had a lively battle with Indians retreating from the siege of Julesburg. James McArdle was the station keeper.

Three historic wagon routes northward from Mud Springs to the vicinity of Courthouse Rock have been identified. After many years of confusion on this point, it now appears that the Pony riders used the left fork to Pumpkinseed Crossing and

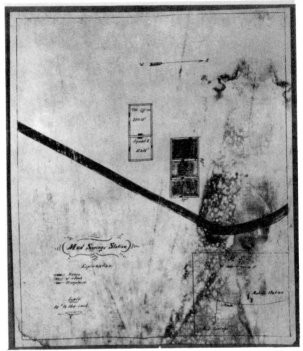

Nebraska State Historical Society

An early plot plan of Mud Springs station drawn by Caspar Collins, a soldier who was killed at the Battle of Platte Bridge.

Courthouse Rock, passing southwest of this landmark. It should be noted that the main trail used by the covered wagons and stage coaches passes to the north of the Rock. Information leading to this discovery may be credited to John Oliver who came

Gregory M. Franzwa

Courthouse Rock

to this neighborhood as a boy in the 1880s and knew James Moore, who had been a Pony rider.

NEBRASKA STATION NO. 33—Courthouse Rock: Most Pony stations were also used as stage stations or trailside ranches, but because of the requirements of an approximate fifteen mile interval, many Pony relay stations had to be built "from scratch." Good examples of this are the unnamed station near Gurley and the Courthouse Rock station. Remains have been identified in the NE corner, SE ¼, Sec. 31, T19N, R50W, five miles south and one and one-fourth miles west of Bridgeport.

Chimney Rock

NEBRASKA STATION NO. 34—Chimney Rock: This formation in the shape of an inverted funnel is one of the most famous of all Oregon Trail landmarks. There was certainly a Pony station between Chimney Rock and the river, but just where is not definitely known. There are two traditional sites, both now obliterated along with emigrant graves by modern road graders and gravel quarrying. John Oliver quoted James Moore to the effect that the Pony station was at Facus Springs, about nine miles northwest of Bridgeport, where the Pony cutoff rejoined the main trail (in Sec. 24, T20N, R52W). Burton's stage station here was north of Chimney rock, ''near a spring on a hill,'' which seems to match the Facus Spring site. The second possible site, which coincides more with the distance given

Don Reynolds-St. Joseph Museum

The Ficklin's Springs marker has been badly vandalized.

in the U. S. mail contract, is further west, being two miles south and one mile west of Bayard (SW Corner, Sec. 5, T20N, R53W).

NEBRASKA STATION NO. 35—Ficklin's Springs: Shumway is in error in calling this "the Scotts Bluff station." The name is blank on the 1861 mail contract. This station was named for Benjamin F. Ficklin, described as "Route Superintendent," with

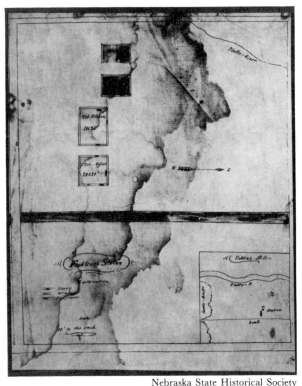

Collins drew this plot plan of the Ficklin's Springs station

managerial charge of the entire line between St. Joe
and Sacramento. The site, with visible surface remains, is marked on State Highway 92, one mile
west of Melbeta in Scotts Bluff County, in NW corner SW ¼, Sec. 13, T21N, R54W. This was another
Pony station built expressly by the men who laid

out the Pony line, and not primarily a stage station. Later, however, like most of the other stations described, it was used as a telegraph station, and for a brief period in 1865 was occupied by troops who dug breast works. In 1871, according to Shumway, the sod structure was appropriated by Mark M. Coad for his open range cattle ranch. Foundation stones are in evidence today.

Burton refers to a ranch called Robidoux's Fort, somewhere between Chimney Rock and the pass at Scotts Bluff (which is clearly identifiable as today's Mitchell Pass). Could this ranch (which is in no way to be compared with Robidoux's Trading Post of 1849 at Robidoux Pass, fifteen miles or so further west) have been the Ficklin's Springs establishment, a Pony Express relay station? It is not unlikely that one of the Robidoux clan of 1849 would have reestablished the name on the main trail in later years.

NEBRASKA STATION NO. 36—Scotts Bluff: The story of old Fort Mitchell, 1864-68, about two and one-half miles northwest of Mitchell Pass at a bend of the North Platte River, has been given to readers of *Nebraska History* in detail. On the other hand, almost nothing is known of this Pony Express station, believed to exist in this same approximate location in 1860-61. When the Eleventh Ohio Cavalry contingent from Fort Laramie built Fort Mitchell, they did not seem to have been aware of a Pony Express station or any previous structure at the site.

Gregory M. Franzwa

Pony riders followed this trail through Mitchell Pass, Scotts Bluff.

At least the military records fail to disclose any such recognition. On the other hand, the "Odometer Book of the Survey for the Fort Kearny, South Pass and Honey Lake Wagon Road, 1857" in the National Archives specifically refers to "old houses, once mail station and trading post of the American Fur Company." In any event, the 1861 mail contract definitely shows a Scotts Bluff station twelve miles west of Ficklin's and fifteen miles east of Horse Creek. Allen has his "U.S. Mail Station" of 1859 as "3 miles west of the Gap." This puts it quite near if not right at the Fort Mitchell site. A granite marker with the circular bronze Pony Express seal of the Oregon Trail Memorial Association, near the

North Platte bridge, commemorates the site.

NEBRASKA STATION NO. 37—Horse Creek: This station is named in the government mail contract and is further identified by Allen in 1859 and Burton in 1860. It may be found in the center of Sec. 25, T23N, R58W, Scotts Bluff County, on the west bank of Horse Creek, about two miles northeast of Lyman. Nine years earlier (1851) the mouth of Horse Creek was the scene of a great peace conference with the Plains Indians.

Burton vividly pictures Horse Creek station, which doubled for stage and Pony Express.

> Presently we dashed over the Little Kiowa Creek, forded the Horse Creek and, enveloped in a cloud of villainous mosquitoes, entered at 8:30 P.M. the station in which we were to pass the night. It was tenanted by one Reynal, a French creole— the son of an old soldier of the Grand Armee, who had settled at St. Louis—a companionable man, but an extortionate; he charged us a florin for every "drink" of his well-watered whiskey. The house boasted of the usual squaw, a wrinkled old dame, who at once began to prepare supper, when we discreetly left the room.

WYOMING STATION NO. 1—Cold Springs: The point where the Oregon Trail-California Road-Pony Express route leaves Nebraska is in a beet field just west of the county road between Lyman and Henry, in Scotts Bluff County.

Little is known of Cold Springs station, believed to be about two miles southeast of Torrington, Wyoming. Contemporary references are lacking. Burton describes this point, about twelve miles west of Horse Creek station, as the place where "in 1854, five Indians, concealing themselves in the bed of a dwarf arroyo, fired upon the mail wagon, killing two drivers and one passenger, and then plundered it of 20,000 dollars."

WYOMING STATION NO. 2—Verdling's Ranch: In 1859 Allen speaks of Beauvais's Ranch; in 1860, to Burton, it was Badean's. The latter name seems most nearly correct since this was certainly the establishment of James Bordeaux, one-time proprietor of the Fort Laramie trading post, eight miles further west. In 1854 he manned a trading post at this point for the American Fur Company when there occurred nearby the misunderstanding with Sioux which led to the extermination of Lieutenant Grattan and twenty-eight soldiers. In 1860 the place consisted of "a single large store, with outhouses full of small half-breeds."

WYOMING STATION NO. 3—Fort Laramie: Fort Laramie, the extensive remains of which are now protected as a National Historic Site, was one of the great military posts of the trans-Mississippi West, flourishing from 1849 to 1890. One might suppose that this would therefore be one of the important Pony Express station of 1860-61. However,

National Park Service

The Sutler's Store at Fort Laramie in 1877.

very little light is thrown on this subject by the meager official records.

There were stations at Bordeaux's (Verdling's) and Ward's (Sand Point), nine miles east and west respectively from the fort. This suggests that there was a Pony station somewhere in the immediate vicinity of the post itself. (As in the case of Fort Kearny, it may not have been within the immediate garrison area.) That the Fort Laramie station was some distance west of the fort area is suggested by this passage from Burton, keeping in mind the fact that for every stage station there were, on the average, two Pony stations:

National Park Service

The post trader's store today.

The hours and halting-places were equally vilely
selected: for instance, at Forts Kearny, Laramie,
and Bridger, the only points where supplies, com-
fort, society, are procurable, a few minutes of
grumbling delay were granted as a favour, and
the passengers were hurried on to some distant
wretched ranch, apparently for the sole purpose
of putting a few dollars into the station-master's
pockets.

Surviving buildings at Fort Laramie which existed in 1860-61 include the imposing frame two-
storied officers' quarters called ''Old Bedlam,'' the

stone magazine, and the adobe-stone sections of the Sutler's Store. The stone portion of the latter structure is known to have been used as a post office in the 1850s when John S. Tutt, post sutler, and Sergeant Leodegar Schnyder served as postmasters. Whether it was the post office in 1860 is unconfirmed. It is known that it served as the post office during the 1870s and the 1880s. In any event, three Fort Laramie buildings still standing saw Pony Express riders come and go. Thus Fort Laramie National Historic Site is one of the principal shrines of the Pony Express route.

IV.
TABULATION OF PONY EXPRESS STATIONS

Identifications and Mileages—St. Joseph, Missouri to Fort Laramie, Wyoming.

1960 Pony Express Research No.	1859 U.S. Mail Station No.	1861 Overland Mail Contract Name	Alternate Spellings, Names or Sites	Contract Miles from Previous Station	Contract Miles from St. Joseph
Missouri No. 1	?	St. Joseph*	—	0	0
Kansas No. 1	—	—	Elwood (E)**, Wathena (E)	—	—
Kansas No. 2	?	Troy	—	15	15
Kansas No. 3	?	Lewis	Cold Springs (E), Valley Home (B)	14	29
Kansas No. 4	3	Kinnekuk*	Kennekuk (R), Kenneykirk (A)	15	44
Kansas No. 5	—	Goteschall	Kickapoo (R), Whitehall (B)	15	59
Kansas No. 6	4	Log Chain	Lockman's (B), Muddy Creek (A), Granada (E)	14	73
Kansas No. 7	5	Seneca*	—	11	84
Kansas No. 8	—	—	Hickory Point (A), Ash Point (E), Laramie Creek (R)	13	—

1960 Pony Express Research No.	1859 U.S. Mail Station No.	1861 Overland Mail Contract Name	Alternate Spellings, Names or Sites	Contract Miles from Previous Station	Contract Miles from St. Joseph
Kansas No. 9	6	Gautard's	Guittards (R) / Vermillion Creek (A)	25	109
Kansas No. 10	7	Marysville*	Big Blue (A) / Palmetto City (B)	12	121
Kansas No. 11	8	Cottonwood	—	10	131
Nebraska No. 1	—	Rock House	Caldwell (R) / Otoe (R)	11	142
Nebraska No. 2	9	Rock Creek	Turkey Creek (A) / Pawnee (R) / Elkhorn (?) / Lodi P.O. (?)	9	151
Nebraska No. 3	—	Virginia City	Grayson's (R) / Whiskey Run (A)	10	161
Nebraska No. 4	10	Big Sandy*	Patterson's (?)	10	171
Nebraska No. 5	—	Millersville	Thompson's (R)	14	185
Nebraska No. 6	—	Kiowa	—	14	199
Nebraska No. 7	11	—Station	Oak Grove (A) / Little Blue (R)	12	211

Nebraska No. 8	12	Liberty Farm*	—	13	224
Nebraska No. 9	—	—	Lone Tree (R)	—	—
			Spring Ranch (N)		
Nebraska No. 10	13	32-Mile Creek	—	25	249
Nebraska No. 11	—	Sand Hill	Summit (R)	18	267
			Water Hole (A)		
Nebraska No. 12	14	Kearney Sta.*	Valley City (B)	8	275
			Hook's (R)		
			Omaha Junction		
Nebraska No. 13	15	Fort Kearney	Fort Kearny	7	282
Nebraska No. 14	—	Platt's	Platte (R)	7	289
			17 Mile pt. (B)		
Nebraska No. 15	—	Garden	Craig (R)	14	303
			Shakespear (?)		
Nebraska No. 16	16	Plum Creek	—	15	318
Nebraska No. 17	17	Willow Island	Willow Bend (A)	15	333
Nebraska No. 18	—	Midway*	Heavy Timber (A)	15	348
			Coldwater R. (B)		
			Pat Mullaly's (?)		
			Lower 96 R. (N)		
Nebraska No. 19	—	Gilman's	—	15	363

1960 Pony Express Research No.	1859 U.S. Mail Station No.	1861 Overland Mail Contract Name	Alternate Spellings, Names or Sites	Contract Miles from Previous Station	Contract Miles from St. Joseph
Nebraska No. 20	—	—	Machette's (N) Upper 96 R. (N)	—	—
Nebraska No. 21	18	Cottonwood Springs	McDonald's R. (N)	16	379
Nebraska No. 22	—	Cold Springs	Junction House (B) Morrow's R. (N) Box Elder (?)	15	394
Nebraska No. 23	—	Fremont Springs*	—	14	408
Nebraska No. 24	19	Dansey's	Buffalo Ranch (C) Elkhorn (R) O'Fallon's (B) Half Way House (B)	11	419
Nebraska No. 25	—	—Station	Alkali Lake (R) Pike's Peak Sta. (C)	15	434
Nebraska No. 26	—	Gill's	Sand Hill (R)	12	446
Nebraska No. 27	20	Diamond Springs*	Beauvais R. (?)	12	458

Colorado No. 1	—	Frontz's Sta.	South Platte (R) Butte Sta. (N)	15	473
Colorado No. 2	—	Julesburg	Overland City (B)	11	484
Nebraska No. 28	—	9-Mile Station	—	9	493
Nebraska No. 29	—	Pole Creek No. 2	Farrell R. (N)	12	505
Nebraska No. 30	—	Pole Creek No. 3	Rouliette Pringle R. (N)	12	517
Nebraska No. 31	—	—	—	—	—
Nebraska No. 32	—	Mud Springs*		26	543
Nebraska No. 33	—	Court House		10	553
Nebraska No. 34	—	Chimney Rock —Station		15	568
Nebraska No. 35	—		Ficklin's Springs	12	580
Nebraska No. 36	23	Scott's Bluff	(Fort Mitchell)	12	592
Nebraska No. 37	—	Horse Creek	—	15	607
Wyoming No. 1	—	Cold Springs	—	12	619
Wyoming No. 2	24	Verdling's Ranch	Bordeaux's R.	13	632
Wyoming No. 3	—	Fort Laramie	Beauvais R.	9	641

*Indicated home stations

**Letters in parenthesis refer to authors cited in chapters II and III

V.
PONY RIDERS IN NEBRASKA

Since official records of the Central Overland are missing, the only evidence for the most part as to the identity of Pony riders consists of interviews with alleged survivors made many decades after the event. Frank Root may have known some of these riders personally (although he doesn't say so). Other writers like Visscher, Bradley, and Chapman could only have depended on the good faith of their informants. Settle found six listings of Pony Express riders, with a total of over 120 names. Only twenty-eight of these, however, appear on all lists. Following is a review of allegations relating to Pony riders in Nebraska, gleaned from Root and Connelley, Chapman, Carter, and Settle (see Chapter II).

Henry Avis, a Fort Laramie resident and veteran of the mail run to Salt Lake City, was hired in 1861 by Joseph Slade to ride between Mud Springs and Horseshoe Station (west of Fort Laramie).

Melvin Baughn, who was later hanged for murder at Seneca, Kansas, at one time rode between Thirty-Two Mile Creek and Fort Kearny.

Jim Beatley, ''whose real name was Foote'' and who had a ''decided preference for wild-half-broken horses,'' operated between Seneca and Big Sandy. He was murdered in 1862 at Farrell's Ranch at Big Sandy.

James W. Brink, according to no less than seven authorities, was either stationed at or rode through Rock Creek Station, and was thus a contemporary of James B. ''Wild Bill'' Hickok.

William Campbell died in 1932 at Stockton, California, alleged then to be the last surviving Pony Express rider. He told Chapman that his relay was along the Platte, between Fort Kearny and Cotton-wood Springs, ''with changes at Plum Creek, Pat Mullaly's Midway, and Gilman Ranch.'' Campbell was six feet tall and 140 pounds, but despite his above-regulation size he was retained because of his tough qualities. He reported various adventures: being chased by wolves, getting thrown by his horse, and once riding twenty-four consecutive hours in zero weather to keep the mail moving.

William A. Cates carried the mail ''from Cottonwood Springs west to Horseshoe Station.'' Since this is a distance of three hundred miles, there is an error somewhere.

James Clark is reported to have ridden between Cottonwood Station (Kansas) and Liberty Farm, a distance of over ninety miles. This is more reasonable.

Richard Cleve is reported by William Campbell to be the rider "opposite" him on his run between Kearny and Cottonwood Springs (also about ninety miles).

Charles Cliff is mistakenly reported by Shumway in his *History of Western Nebraska* to have ridden in the vicinity of Scotts Bluff. "On his return he was attacked by Indians in Mitchell Gap, and when he arrived at Scott's Bluff station he had three bullets in his body and twenty-seven through his clothes." Root and Connelley have him riding between Mud Springs and Scotts Bluff all right, but Settle says he ran between St. Joseph and Seneca and was bored there by the lack of excitement. Both sources contradict Shumway on the Pony Express Indian attack, stating that this attack did not occur until 1863, while Cliff was freighting with ox teams.

William F. Cody, the one and only "Buffalo Bill," claims that at fifteen years of age he was employed as a Pony Express rider and given a "a short 45 mile run from Julesburg to the west." Subsequently he reported to Slade at Horseshoe Station and rode between Red Buttes and Three Crossings, with alleged herioc feats climaxed by a 384 mile run made necessary when another rider was killed by Indians. There are many discrepancies in the Cody legend, not the least of which is the tender age at which he was employed.

[An article in the spring 1985 issue of *Kansas History* has proved that all Cody's claims of being a Pony Express rider are false. He was never more than a messenger boy.]

Frank Helvey's claim to being a Pony Express rider is expressed in the reminiscence of his daughter published in *Nebraska History* 21, no. 1 (Jan-March 1940): 22. the Helvey family had a ranch on the Little Sandy in Jefferson County. Frank Helvey claimed to be a substitute rider.

Martin Hogan, Julesburg to Mud Springs.

David Robert Jay, Big Sandy to Marysville. Jay lived until 1930. Settle says he was hired "in spite of the fact he was not yet fourteen years of age." Perhaps Buffalo Bill at fifteen was not too young after all. But what about that twenty year age rule?

William D. Jenkins, at Big Sandy.

Jack Keetley, like Robert Campbell, was one of the few who rode the Pony eighteen months, from start to finish. He handled the Marysville-Big Sandy stretch. He was another marathon rider, once going 340 miles in thirty-one hours. "He was taken from the saddle sound asleep."

Jim Moore rode from Midway to Julesburg. He made another famous ride, of 280 miles, in something less than fifteen hours when relief riders were not available. This achievement is commemorated by a plaque on the surviving Midway station.

Theodore Rand, also known as "Little Yank," took the first herd of horses out of St. Joseph to stock the line. He is reputed to have had the run between

Cottonwood Springs and Julesburg. He is also identified with Box Elder.

Don C. Rising, at sixteen, rode between Log Chain and Marysville, later between Big Sandy and Fort Kearny. His father was the station master at Log Chain.

Alexander Topence was a bullwhacker for Russell, Majors, and Waddell, and an employee of the Butterfield Overland Mail before he was hired, at age twenty-four, "as a rider in Lewis' Division." Carter has him going westward from Fort Kearny.

Henry Wallace was "given the run from Big Sandy to Liberty Farm," a little over fifty miles.

Joseph B. Wintle is another rider between Fort Kearny and Cottonwood Springs. He reports having once ridden 110 miles in five hours with ten changes of horses. He had several brushes with Indians.

Luther C. North, the famous Indian fighter of Columbus, Nebraska, told Chapman that he tried to get a job as a Pony Express rider at Fort Kearny as a boy but was turned down because he was too young. In view of the number of teen-agers who did apparently obtain such employment, it appears that there was a distinct lack of uniformity in the application of the age-twenty-or-over policy. Perhaps some of the applicants were not above a little harmless prevarication in an age when birth certificates had not yet been invented.

Other Western Books Published or Marketed by The Patrice Press

These books may be purchased by direct mail.
Order from:
The Patrice Press
1701 South Eighth St., St. Louis, MO 63104
There is a $2.95 shipping and handling charge for the first book and a 95-cent charge for each additional book. Missourians please add 6.1% sales tax.
You may call toll-free to place your order:
1-800-367-9242

AMERICAN HISTORY

Exploring the American West: 1803-1879. William Goetzmann. 128 pages. Paper, $7.95.

Kansas in Maps. Robert W. Baughman. 104 pages. Cloth, $14.95.

The Beginning of the West. Louise Barry. 1296 pages. Cloth, $14.75.

The Latter-day Saints' Emigrants' Guide. Wm. Clayton; Stanley B. Kimball, Ph.D., ed. 107 pages. Paper, $9.95, ISBN: 0-935284-27-3.

Old Utah Trails. William B. Smart. 136 pages. Paper, $17.95. Cloth, $28.95.

The Overland Migrations. David Lavender. 111 pages. Paper, $7.95.

THE OREGON-CALIFORNIA TRAIL

Fort Laramie. David Lavender. 159 pages. Paper, $8.95.

Fort Vancouver. David Lavender. 143 pages. Paper, $8.95.

Forty-niners. Archer Butler Hulbert. 340 pages. Paper, $14.95.

The Great Platte River Road. Merrill J. Mattes. 583 pages. Cloth, $36.95. Paper, $16.95.

Historic Sites Along the Oregon Trail. Aubrey L. Haines. 439 pages. Cloth, $24.95, ISBN: 0-935284-50-8. Paper, $12.95, ISBN: 0-935284-51-6.

Historic Sites and Markers Along the Mormon and Other Great Western Trails. Stanley B. Kimball. 320 pages. Cloth, $37.95. Paper, $15.95.

Maps of the Oregon Trail. Gregory M. Franzwa. 292 pages. Cloth, $24.95, ISBN: 0-935284-30-3. Paper, $14.95, ISBN: 0-935284-32-X. Looseleaf, $27.95, ISBN: 0-935284-31-1.

Old Oregon Trail Map. 16″ X 24″. $2.95.

The Oregon Trail Revisited. Gregory M. Franzwa. 419 pages. Cloth, $14.95, ISBN: 0-935284-57-5. Paper, $12.95, ISBN: 0-935284-58-3.

Overland to California with the Pioneer Line: The Gold Rush Diary of Bernard J. Reid. Mary McDougall Gordon, ed. 246 pages. Paper, $14.95.

The Plains Across. John D. Unruh, Jr. 364 pages. Paper, $12.95.

Platte River Road Narratives. Merrill J. Mattes. 672 pages, 8½″ X 11″. Cloth, $95.

Pump on the Prairie. Musetta Gilman. 223 pages. Paper, $12.95.

Scotts Bluff. Merrill J. Mattes. 64 pages. Paper, $2.45.

Trail of the First Wagons Over the Sierra Nevada. Charles K. Graydon. 81 pages. Paper, $12.95, ISBN: 0-935284-47-8.

To the Land of Gold and Wickedness: The 1848-59 Diary of Lorena Hays. Jeanne Hamilton Watson, ed. 496 pages. Cloth, $27.95, ISBN: 0-935284-53-2.

The Wake of the Prairie Schooner. Irene D. Paden. 514 pages. Cloth, $24.95, ISBN: 0-935284-40-0. Paper, $12.95, ISBN: 0-935284-38-9.

Whitman Mission. Erwin N. Thompson. 92 pages. Paper, $4.45.

THE SANTA FE TRAIL

Following the Santa Fe Trail. Marc Simmons, Ph.D. 214 pages. Paper, $12.95.

Images of the Santa Fe Trail. Gregory M. Franzwa. 114 photographs. Cloth, $29.95, ISBN: 0-935284-60-5. Paper, $19.95, ISBN: 0-935284-61-3.

Impressions of The Santa Fe Trail: A Contemporary Diary. Gregory M. Franzwa. 207 pages. Cloth, $14.95, ISBN: 0-935284-62-1. Paper, $9.95, ISBN: 0-935284-63-X.

Land of Enchantment: Memoirs of Marian Russell along the Santa Fe Trail. Garnet M. Brayer, ed. 163 pages. Paper, $12.95.

Maps of the Santa Fe Trail. Gregory M. Franzwa. Cloth, $24.95, ISBN: 0-935284-68-0. Looseleaf, $29.95, ISBN: 0-935284-69-9.

The Santa Fe Trail: The National Park Service 1963 Historic Sites Survey. William E. Brown. 221 pages. Cloth, $17.95, ISBN: 0-935284-64-8.

Two wonderful associations to enhance enjoyment of the trails:

The Santa Fe Trail Association

Your membership will:
- ☐ Help with efforts to preserve the remaining ruts of the Santa Fe Trail and associated historic sites
- ☐ Bring you four thrilling issues of *Wagon Tracks* each year, with news of the association and the trail
- ☐ Enable you to attend the conventions and conferences of the association, where you can:
  - ☐ enjoy the field trips out on the trail
  - ☐ hear thrilling papers about the trail, and
  - ☐ enjoy the camaradarie of fellow trail students and scholars

OREGON-CALIFORNIA TRAILS ASSOCIATION

Your membership will:
- ☐ Help save the remaining traces of the trails and related historic sites
- ☐ Bring you four issues of the *Overland Journal* and four issues of *News From the Plains* each year
- ☐ Enable you to attend OCTA conventions in historic trail cities each year, featuring:
  - ☐ field trips to important trails sites
  - ☐ wonderful slide shows and papers on the trail and its history, and
  - ☐ the companionship of new and interesting trail friends

**For a free membership application
to both trails associations,
call toll-free: 1-800-367-9242**